The Awesome Restoration
of the Sephardic Jews!

VISION
NEGEV

DOMINIQUAE
BIERMAN, PHD

AUTHOR OF *THE IDENTITY THEFT*

First Printing September 2012, Second Printing June 2021

Paperback ISBN: 978-1-953502-43-8
E-Book ISBN: 978-1-953502-44-5

Published by Zions Gospel Press | shalom@zionsgospel.com

52 Tuscan Way, Ste 202-412

St. Augustine, FL, 32092, USA

Kad-Esh MAP Ministries | www.kad-esh.org | info@kad-esh.org

ZIONS GOSPEL
PRESS

Acknowledgments

To the God of Israel and His unfailing Word and Holy Spirit that has led me in a never-ending path of discovery. To the Latino members of my Congregation from 1998, *Kehilat HarTsion* that while existing in South Tel Aviv until 2004, they taught me much and especially how to love my own Sephardic Roots that led me to rediscover the importance of the Negev and its divinely appointed heirs.

And the exiles from Yerushalayim in S'farad, will repossess the cities in the Negev.
OBADIAH 20B (CJB)

CONTENTS

INTRODUCTION

Though I am a Sephardic Jew (my Jewish ancestors were expelled from Spain during the Spanish Inquisition in 1492) and I also have the privilege of being a licensed tour guide of Israel since 1984, I am far from being an authority on the Negev. Some people call me "Prophet" and if so, then I am qualified by the Almighty to cast vision towards what I consider to be the most important piece of Land besides Jerusalem in the world! The Negev is the South Desert of Israel starting from south of Ashkelon (the Northern Gate of the Negev) and ending in the City of Eilat on the Red Sea (The Southern Gate of the Negev). It covers up to 55% of the land allotted to modern day Israel. Most of it dry and desolate, a vast wilderness of 4600 square miles, only to be interrupted by the Biblical and Patriarchal City of Abraham, Beer Sheba. Others like Dimona and Mitspe Ramon are defying all heat and abrasiveness of the elements and are still there surviving and reviving. Culminating in the miraculous apparition, the City of Eilat, that has become the "hottest" holiday resort of Israel and the Middle East, both because of its climate (all the way up to 50 degrees centigrade in the summer) and because of its amazing beauty!

Our national Israeli Poet, late HayimNachmanBialik, said in one of his poems:

The human being is shaped in the likeness of the landscape of his home land.

If so, I can explain my romance with the Negev-Desert of Israel, being a Jew from the Tribe of Judah that comprises the region from Jerusalem, to Beer Sheva to the Red Sea, my ancestors were from here. But not only the past speaks to the depths of my soul, but the present and especially the future of this Promised Land. The Biblical Promise says that the Jews that were captive in Spain, which is Sepharad will possess the cities of the Negev (South). (Obadiah 20).

My ancestors lived in Sepharad until 1492 and they were captives in the sense of being in exile far from their homeland, Israel. However, there were many other captives, also Jewish that became captive to the Catholic Religious system in order to escape the draconic orders of the Spanish Inquisition. They converted some time willingly and mostly by force and thus lost their Jewish Identity becoming staunch Catholics and sometimes hating everything Jewish. Many of them kept Jewish traditions underground for fear of the Auto de Fe and the terrible bonfires that ensued. Many thousands lost their lives on those bonfires for keeping the Shabbat, celebrating Passover, reading the Torah or eating Kosher.

Today, statistics say that there are about 60 million descendants of those Sephardic Jews that became Catholic and many of them are waking up to their roots - their Jewish Roots. They are also shaped in the likeness of their homeland, the Negev and they are yearning to return to it and fulfill the Obadiah 20 Prophecy,

And the exiles from Yerushalayim in S'farad, will repossess the cities in the Negev. Obadiah 20b

CHAPTER ONE

MY SHEEP

On my 40th birthday, the 5th of September of 1998, I received a special gift from the Almighty. I received the pastorate of an entire Hispanic Congregation of foreign workers in the hardest place of Tel Aviv-namely, South Tel Aviv, an area full of drug addiction and prostitution. For some reason, YHVH has always given me the South! I was born in Chile, the Southern Gate of all of South America! Right before starting the pastorate in South Tel Aviv, I was leading *Kehilat HarKadosh*, the Congregation of the Holy Mountain in the South Gate of Jerusalem, Arnona-Talpiot not far from Beth Lechem.

There, I received the instruction from the Holy Spirit to establish the Evening and the Morning sacrifice of praise and that we did, culminating in my husband and I moving to pastor in South Tel Aviv! From the South Gate of Jerusalem to the South Gate of Tel Aviv! About 10 years later, at the end of 2007, the Holy Spirit spoke to me "out of the blue" to relocate all the way to the South

Gate of Israel; that is Eilat on the Red Sea where we are at present as I am writing this book and where we have established the Eilat Prayer Tower.

When we came to pastor in South Tel Aviv among the foreign and mostly "illegal workers" (later I learnt that the only illegal in this earth is satan!), I spoke to my Father in Heaven, my "boss" and said:

"You know Lord that these people are illegal here; they have no work visas and they have overstayed many years in Israel. So, after my first sermon about righteousness and holiness, they will all leave the congregation because I will tell them to get right with the authorities."

To my astonishing surprise, Elohim did not seem to be too impressed with my self-righteous sermon! He answered me in a "snappy" tone of voice:

"These are *My* sheep, now what are you going to do?"

Well, I was not expecting that answer! The fear of Yah (God) gripped me and I quickly said: "If these are *your* sheep, then I will pastor them!" And pastor I did for nearly 5 solid years until most of them were deported by the Israeli authorities, leaving many broken hearts behind, including ours! Many, many of them got born again and filled with the Holy Spirit under our hands! Many miracles happened in Levanda 2, South Tel Aviv, where the legendary *Kehilat HarTsion* was established, called by many local Jews "The Little Synagogue".

They could pinpoint to the fact that our worship was much more Jewish than Christian, celebrating the Shabbats and the

biblical feasts and yet professing the name of Yeshua and mani-
festing the power of the Ruach Hakodesh (Holy Spirit) to heal
and deliver mightily! Prayers started at 5 AM in our Kehila (congregation) every day! The languages most spoken were Spanish,
Hebrew, English, Russian and sometimes even Chinese and of
course, Tongues! These were powerful days of visitation of the
Holy Spirit and of many anointed international servants of Elohim that graced our pulpit very often! One day, a cloud filled the
sanctuary and everyone that passed under that cloud received a
"shower of gold" liquid and "dust!"

Sometimes, the "sheep" from other congregations would sneak
into our services just to get filled with the Ruach (Spirit) to go
back to their congregations carrying a precious cargo of revival!
Of course, the work did not go uncontested as there were enough
Hispanic pastors and ministers that did their best to torpedo
us for various reasons and especially me being a woman Pastor
and teaching these Christians (mostly of Catholic background!)
about the Jewish roots of the faith! There were some painful
days when many of "my" sheep were visited by the said pastors,
warning them to leave the congregation! Nevertheless, with faith,
sacrifice and prophetic intercession, we established a congregation
of revival and holiness in the midst of the filthiest area of Israel.

Some-times, Israelis would come to the meetings because they
heard the praise music from the windows! Our Spanish-Hebrew
praise spoke to the hearts of many and especially to the Heart of
our Abba, who had said to me:

These are *My* sheep, now what are you going to do?

It took me many more years to figure out exactly what He meant by that phrase- MY Sheep. I thought to myself, that all believers are His sheep and He knew that among the Hispanic Catholics and Evangelicals of South Tel Aviv, there were many of His sheep! A few years later, He began to reveal to me about the restoration of a large portion of Israel, lost to the Spanish Inquisition since 1492 and even earlier; these were the Sephardic (Spanish) Jews! It was then that I fully understood that "MY Sheep" was much wider and deeper than I thought!

YHVH meant: These are my Jewish (lost) sheep, now what will you do? They are not "legal" by the laws of modern day Israel but they are legal by My biblical standards. I am restoring them to their identity and to their Promised Land!

And the exiles from Yerushalayim in S'farad, will repossess the cities in the Negev.

Obadiah 20b CJB

CHAPTER TWO

RETURNING TO TOLEDO

In 1994, I received an instruction from the Holy Spirit that shook my being: I want you to go to Toledo, Spain from where your ancestors were expelled in 1492 and the Spanish Inquisition began.

I had never been there before! Obeying the Holy Spirit promptly, my husband and I boarded a flight from Israel to Madrid, Spain. After traveling to Toledo less than two hours away, we were received by a local Messianic Pastor who acted as our guide. Already from afar, I was moved to tears while arriving to the City that is called "The Second Jerusalem." Even its contour reminds you of the Old City of Jerusalem with the only difference that in Toledo most everything is built with red bricks and in the Holy City, it is white lime stone. Red bricks indeed a prophetic picture of the quantity of Jewish blood that ran through this city from 1492. Surrounded by Rio Tajo, the infamous river that saw so many Jews smashed against its rocks! I felt as if I was coming home after 500 years of absence; my soul, my spirit and everything in me was going through a revolution of emotions. In the midst of this dramatic experience, the Holy Spirit spoke to me:

Go to the Major Synagogue of Toledo to pray.

"Lord," I said, "How do you want me to find synagogues here? The Spanish destroyed all the synagogues or transformed them into churches, many, many churches! There is not one synagogue left in Toledo!" "I will lead you" said the still small voice of the Ruach and thus I started to walk as the Holy Spirit was gently leading me and whispering to my ears clear, very clear directions: To the right, to the left, now go straight...Right next to me and behind me followed my husband, Rabbi Baruch and the Messianic pastor. We found ourselves in front of a massive stone building, a historic tourist site: The Church of Santa Maria La Blanca! The Holy Spirit, told me:

Here you are! Go buy tickets and go in!

We paid the fee and went in finding ourselves in a typical Catholic Church, with the typical Iconostasis or partition full of icons of dead saints and figures of the virgin. Except my eyes caught a surprising sight! Right on the floor of what could have been the place for the Ark of the Torah scrolls, had this been a Jewish synagogue before, there was an ornate floor, full of 14-15 century style Magen David (David stars). I was so excited and all of us were moved to praise and prayer. This had been the Major Synagogue of Toledo prior to the expulsion after all! The Holy Spirit told me to pray and repent for the sins of my ancestors the, Sephardic Jews. I went on my knees on the "Jewish floor" and started to pray and ask forgiveness from Abba for all the sins committed, including Kabbalah and the rejecting of Messiah. As I finished my prayers of repentance on behalf of my ancestors, all of a sudden, a heavy mourning fell upon me and I started to wail from the depth of my being, oblivious that I was in a public place and that people were coming and going incessantly. The two men that accompanied me knelt beside me as I wailed for about 45 minutes or more! As I cried inconsolably, I asked the Father: "Why am I crying like this?" He said: "You are mourning for all your family that was murdered inside of this synagogue." All of a sudden, someone turned the lights off and motioned us to leave. Visiting time was over, the place was going to close!

Still shaken, pale and with tears streaming down my eyes, supported by my husband and the pastor, I left the church-synagogue and was stopped at the entrance door by a stern looking woman. She was a Catholic nun dressed in civilian clothes and she asked me a question: "Visitors that saw you inside were asking what you were doing in there?" Her face looked hard and bitter. I looked at her directly in the eyes and said: "I am a Sephardic Jew and your people murdered my family and expelled the remnant of us from Spain, but because I have met Yeshua, the Jewish Messiah whom you call Jesus and He has forgiven me of so much, I also have forgiven your people."

There was a tense moment as tears began to stream down the eyes of this stern woman, her face softened and we both fell into the arms of the other sobbing, a Catholic and a Sephardic Jew in an embrace of forgiveness and love, with a hint of hope of promise for the reconciliation of both our peoples!

While in the Church-Synagogue and repenting for the sins of my Sephardic ancestors, I also called them prophetically to return home to Israel and to the God of Israel. I thought that I was calling those Spanish Jews like me that did not forsake our Jewish identity and were forced to leave Spain. I was not aware at all that I was actually calling prophetically a much larger group of people that had forsaken their identity as Jews in order to appease the authorities of the Spanish Inquisition! These were called later the Conversos, Marranos and sometimes also Crypto Jews! Little did I know that though lost, yet the Almighty had kept track on them and that latest statistics informed us that there are about 60 million descendants of them! And I was calling them back home, to Israel and to be cleansed from all idolatry!

> For I will take you from the nations, gather you from all the lands and bring you into your own land. Then I will sprinkle clean water on you, and you will be clean; I will cleanse you from all your filthiness and from all your idols.
>
> Ezekiel 36:24-25

CHAPTER THREE

BEN GURYON'S NEGEV VISION

"The Negev is one of the Jewish Nation's safe havens"
DAVID BEN-GURION, ISRAEL'S FIRST PRIME MINISTER

O ur first Prime Minister, David Ben Gurion, was a man of great insight and vision as fitting for the first Prime Minister of Israel after 2000 years of exile! Already at the offset of the Jewish State, he saw that the Negev is a great asset to Israel. He predicted that the future of Israel (just like its past during Abraham's times) is depending on the settling of the Negev. The Prophet Isaiah predicted that the Negev would bloom and the desert would rejoice!

The desert and the dry land will be glad; the 'Aravah' will rejoice and blossom like the lily.

Isaiah 35:1 CJB

The Story of *Kibbutz Revivim*

Kibbutz Revivim (which means "drops of soft rain") is the mother of all Kibbutzim (community farms) in the Negev. It was the first one to defy the terrible heat and dryness of the region. Its young pioneers established it in 1946 and tilled the dry and thirsty land with superhuman effort. While visiting the Kibbutz, the guide told me a most astounding story. In 1947, a delegation from the League of Nations (UN of today) visited the Negev in order to decide whether to allot it to the newly created country of Jordan or the emerging Jewish State. While approaching Kibbutz Revivim, they saw what they considered to be a "mirage!" Out in the distance, they could detect a large field of blooming Gladiola Flowers! Impossible! They said to themselves, "Gladiola Flowers cannot grow in this desert." They reached this fantastic field and thought that the Jews were trying to trick them and they just placed pots of gladiolas on the ground to "make believe" as if gladiolas could grow in that dry sand. They started digging under the flowers and they found no pots but rather roots. These dainty beautiful flowers were indeed growing in dry desert sand! This was the determining factor of their decision! If these Jews can make gladiolas bloom in this forsaken, desolate place, sure they can have the Negev!

The Kibbutz members go ahead to tell that this was in fact the only time that this gladiola flowers bloomed right before the eyes of the delegation that would determine the future of the Negev! Obviously, the God of Israel had His say! The Negev is Holy Land, Promised Land and it belongs to Israel!

Kibbutz Revivim today is suffering from harassment. Overnight, thousands of Bedouin squatters surrounded the Kibbutz and settled there in a menacing way. They refuse to leave and they are often stealing sheep, goats and other vital equipment from the Kibbutz members. The Israeli police have refused to bring order to this distressful situation since it could cause a clash with the Bedouins that have become more and more radical Moslems. Kibbutz Revivim and all of the Negev needs our prayers to stop Islam and to provoke an urgent settling of the region with Jewish people that have the vision and the desire to pay the price to possess thus dry land and make it bloom!

Prophet Obadiah connected the right people to this very dry piece of biblical land. In fact, the only people that will cause the fulfillment of the Prophecy in Isaiah 35, the blooming of the desert of Israel.

And the exiles from Yerushalayim in S'farad, will repossess the cities in the Negev.

Obadiah 20 (CJB)

Those Sephardic (Spanish) Jews that fell captive to the Spanish Inquisition in Spain, they are the natural heirs that this desolate

15

and very promising piece of holy land is waiting for! In fact, until they return en masse, the Negev is in danger of being lost to Islam. The Bedouin (Nomadic Arab tribes) population of the Negev has been dramatically increasing and this on purpose, in order to disconnect the Negev from the rest of Israel! They are relocating their people from other areas of Israel in order to squat and take more land illegally in order to prevent 55% of Israel's land to actually be Israeli! It is a matter of a few years, to have a Moslem takeover of this area! While the whole world is concerned with terror from Gaza and the nuclear threat from Iran, there is a steady revolution of takeover of more than half of the land of Israel and the authorities have been too "anemic" to stop it!

On top of it, there have been too many obstacles for the Conversos, the Anusim, and the descendants of the Sephardic Jews to actually return to Israel's bosom. Many of them are ready and eager to come but have not been given the green light by the Israeli government unless they go through a harrowing process of conversion to Orthodox Judaism that is neither necessary nor productive. There is no doubt a need for reeducation and restoration of their Jewish roots but this can be done with a good education program without any need for Orthodox conversions. The government of Israel will find itself between "the rock and the hard place", it is either the Moslems who hate the Jews or the Sephardic Jews that have been disconnected from their Jewish roots but are eager to reconnect, make Alyah (return to the Land) and work hard to make the Negev bloom.

Say to those with anxious heart, "Take courage, fear not. Behold, your God will come with vengeance; the recompense of God will come,but He will save you." Then the eyes of the blind will be opened and the ears of the deaf will be unstopped. Then the lame will leap like a deer, and the tongue of the mute will shout for joy. For waters will break forth in the wildernessand streams in the Aravah. And the ransomed of YHVH will returnand come with joyful shouting to Zion, with everlasting joy upon their heads. They will find gladness and joy, and sorrow and sighing will flee away.

Isaiah 35: 4-6,10

CHAPTER FOUR

EILAT ON THE RED SEA

The South Gate of the Negev

I will fix your boundary from the Red Sea to the sea of the Philistines, and from the wilderness to the River Euphrates; for I will deliver the inhabitants of the land into your hand, and you will drive them out before you.
EXODUS 23:31

E ilat is Israel's southernmost city, a busy port as well as a popular resort, located at the northern tip of the Red Sea, on the Gulf of Aqaba. Home to 60,000 people, the city is part of the Southern Negev Desert, at the southern end of the Aravah. The city is adjacent to the Egyptian village of Taba to the south, the Jordanian port city of Aqaba to the east, and within sight of Saudi Arabia to the south-east, across the gulf. Eilat's arid desert climate and low humidity is moderated by proximity to a warm sea. Temperatures often exceed 40 °C (104°F) in summer, and 21°C (70°F) in winter, while water temperatures range between 20 and 26°C (68 and 79°F). Eilat averages up to 360 sunny days a year. The city's beaches, nightlife and desert landscapes make it a popular destination for domestic and international tourism.

The deliverers will ascend Mount Zion to judge the mountain of Esau, and the kingdom will be YHVH's.

Obadiah 21

The Word of God tells us that the End time battle is between Jacob and Esau. The name of Esau is Edom, meaning *red* because he sold his birthright to Jacob, his younger brother for a stew of *red* lentils. Eilat is in the border with the land of Edom. That is why the Red Sea in Hebrew is called *Ha Yam Haadom*, "the Sea of Edom." The mountains across the City of Eilat on the side of the now Jordanian Aqaba (the site of ancient Eilat in the Bible) are called the Mountains of Edom. That is the view from the Eilat Prayer Tower, established in 2009 as a Watchman over the City of Eilat and its surrounding borders! In the context of Obadiah 21, we have Obadiah 20 that promises that the deliverers of the Negev are the Sephardic Jews that were captives to the Catholic Inquisition in Spain.

And the exiles of Jerusalem who are in Sepharad will possess the cities of the Negev.

Obadiah 20b

These possessors of the Negev will deliver Israel from "Esau" that has been persecuting Jacob since biblical times! Esau is Edom and Eilat, originally allotted to the Tribe of Judah is over the land of Edom. In ancient times, there were always quarrels between Edom and Israel concerning this area. The Edomites claimed it and yet it was given to the Tribe of Judah by Elohim Himself.

And all the people of Judah took Uzziah, who was sixteen years old, and made him king in the place of his father Amaziah.He built Eloth and restored it to Judah after the king slept with his fathers.

2 Chronicles 26:2

However, because of this ancient feud and by reason of it being disconnected from the rest of Israel by the vast Negev Desert and Aravah, many religious Jews considered Eilat as "heathen" and not Holy Land! It is very interesting to note that since we established the Eilat Prayer Tower in Eilat, overlooking the Mountains of Edom we have declared Eilat as The Holy City of Eilat. And now the religious, orthodox Jews seem to have adopted the city and they now include it in their prayers as *holy*. That is the power of prophetic declaration!

The Spirit of Esau that is none other than the Spirit of 'Amalek (the grandson of Esau see Genesis 26:12!) will be defeated and is being defeated in Eilat through prayer, worship and sacrifice!

> ADONAI said to Moshe, "Write this in a book to be remembered, and tell it to Y'hoshua: I will completely blot out any memory of 'Amalek from under heaven and said, "Because their hand was against the throne of Yah, ADONAI will fight 'Amalek generation after generation."
>
> Exodus 17:14, 16 (CJB)

Amalek attacked the weak, the children and the women. All Islamic terror functions under a spirit of Amalek!

> Remember what 'Amalek did to you on the road as you were coming out of Egypt, how he met you by the road, attacked those in the rear, those who were exhausted and straggling behind when you were tired and weary. He did not fear God. Therefore, when Adonai your God has given you rest from all your surrounding enemies in the land Adonai your God is giving you as your inheritance to possess, you are to blot out all memory of 'Amalek from under heaven. Don't forget!
>
> Deuteronomy 25:17-19 (CJB)

Amalek has always arisen to annihilate Israel, all the way from the battle in the desert fought by Joshua (Exodus 17), to ancient Persia through wicked Haman (Book of Esther) and modern Israel through the Moslem nations surrounding Eilat! In Eilat, we can subdue the principality of Amalek at its home base, the place of birth of his grandfather, Esau. The Word of Yah (God) says that Amalek dwells in the Negev!

'Amalek lives in the area of the Negev; the Hitti, the Y'vusi and the Emori live in the hills; and the Kena'ani live by the sea and alongside the Yarden."

Numbers 13:29 (CJB)

By defeating Esau in Eilat and over the Mountains of Edom, we can rid the Negev from the influence of Amalek and fill the Negev with Sephardic Jews that will become the deliverers of Israel! Many prophecies in years past said that "The Revival of Israel will start from the Spanish speakers!"

Enemies must be defeated at the gate and Eilat is the South gate of the Negev and of all of Israel!

He will also be a spirit of justicefor whoever sits as a judge, and a source of strength for thoserepelling enemy attacks at the gate.

Isaiah 28:6

Biblical Eilat

Eilat is first mentioned in the Hebrew bible in the Book of Exodus. The first six stations of the Exodus are in Egypt. The seventh is the crossing of the Red Sea and the ninth–thirteenth are in and around Eilat, after the exodus from Egypt and crossing the Red Sea. Station twelve refers to a dozen campsites in and around Timna in Modern Israel near Eilat. When King David conquered Edom, which up to then had been a common border of Edom and Median, he took over Eilat, the border city shared by them as well. The commercial port city and copper based industrial center were maintained by Egypt until reportedly rebuilt by Solomon at a location known as Ezion-Geber (I Kings 9:26). In 2 Kings 14:21–22: "And all the people of Judah took Azariah, who was sixteen years old, and made him king in the room of his father Amaziah. He built *Elath*, and restored it to Judah, after that the king slept among his fathers." And again in 2 Kings 16:6: "At that time Rezin king of Aram recovered *Elath* to Aram, and drove the Jews from *Elath*; and the Edomites came to *Elath*, and dwelt there, unto this day. " (Wikipedia)

It is from here that the twelve Tribes of Israel made their way into the Promised Land; here they camped and moved under the Cloud of Glory and the Pillar of Fire!

So, we passed beyond our brothers the sons of Esau, who live in Seir, away from the Aravah road, away from Elath and from Ezion-geber. And we turned and passed through by the way of the wilderness of Moab.

Deuteronomy 2:8

Hence God led the people around by the way of the wilderness to the Red Sea; and the sons of Israel went up in martial array from the land of Egypt.

Exodus 13:18

YHVH was going before them in a pillar of cloud by day to lead them on the way, and in a pillar of fire by night to give them light, that they might travel by day and by night.He did not take away the pillar of cloud by day, nor the pillar of fire by night, from before the people.

Exodus 13:21-22

It is in the same waters of the Red Sea that Israel saw its greatest and most documented historical miracle! The crossing of the Red Sea on dry ground of over one million Israelites!

Then Moses stretched out his hand over the sea; and the Lord swept the sea back by a strong east wind all night and turned the sea into dry land, so the waters were divided.The sons of Israel went through the midst of the sea on the dry land, and the waters were like a wall to them on their right hand and on their left.

Exodus 14:21-22

All the enemies of Israel drown at the Red sea! Eilat on the Red Sea is the gate of defeat for all the enemies of Israel!

So Moses stretched out his hand over the sea, and the sea returned to its normal state at daybreak, while the Egyptians were fleeing right into it; then the Lord overthrew the Egyptians in the midst of the sea. The waters returned and covered the chariots and the horsemen, even Pharaoh's entire army that had gone into the sea after them; not even one of them remained.

Exodus 14:27-28

And it is not far from here that the Torah, the Ten Commandments, the righteous foundation for any nation to thrive was given to the people of Israel! Eilat's Southern border (Taba) is with the Sinai desert and Egypt!

When He had finished speaking with him upon Mount Sinai, He gave Moses the two tablets of the testimony, tablets of stone, written by the finger of God.

Exodus 31:18

The area of Eilat is one of the most important biblical areas in all of Israel! It is also one of the most beautiful regions and cities in the world! Every year, about 250,000 divers frequent the famous Eilat Coral Reefs, one of the Seven Wonders of the world according to UNESCO (*United Nations Educational, Scientific and Cultural Organization*). It is also the bird-watching paradise of all nations as all species of birds like to stop in Eilat to refuel during their long journey crossing continents. The sky of Eilat is filled with all sorts of species of birds and especially large quantities of eagles!

We also have "snow birds" escaping the cold winter months in Scandinavia and Europe! Quantities of Fins, Norwegians and others grace the city during winter months. Winter in Eilat is very short and it is mostly like summer elsewhere!

The Royal Port

King Solomon also built a fleet of ships in Ezion-geber, which is near Eloth on the shore of the Red Sea, in the land of Edom.

1 Kings 9:26

Eilat is also the gate of trade and wealth with Africa, Europe and Asia and all the way to the Solomon Islands in the Pacific! The famous Queen of Sheba visited King Solomon bearing lavish gifts, entering into Israel through the royal port of King Solomon- the Port of Eilat!

Never again did such abundance of spices come in as that which the queen of Sheba gave King Solomon.

1 Kings 10:10

Most probably, she left pregnant bearing Solomon's seed to Africa where Jewish blood was mixed with African! She entered and exited Israel with all her entourage from the Royal Port City of Eilat.

King Solomon gave to the Queen of Sheba all her desire which she requested, besides what he gave her according to his royal bounty. Then she turned and went to her own land together with her servants.

1 Kings 10:13

King Uzziah and Jehoshaphat also made Eilat their Royal Ports! (2 Kings 22:48, 2 Chronicles 26:2)

The Tribe of Judah's land portion starts South of Jerusalem, includes the Negev and ends in Eilat! Eilat's biblical names are Eilat/Eloth and Ezion Geber. The origin of the name is uncertain but it could come from ayelet, which is the name for deer. In some translations, they connect the name Eilat with the name Elath, which is the name for the Canaanite goddess, Ashera. I prefer to connect the name with ayelet, which in Hebrew carries the same letters as Eilat namely Aleph, Yot, Lamed, Taf. Only that it is a double Yot.

Yot is the letter that starts the Holy name of YHVH and on its own it means YHVH-

Today, Eilat is the center for international conventions and sport events, music and jazz festivals and very soon, it will become the center of worship to the Living God!

Most of Israel comes to unwind and unburden from stress and to take their holidays in Eilat. If you want to meet Israelis from all walks of life and from all cities of Israel, come to Eilat and you will find them!

Since Eilat is in the Land of Edom area, the word Edom or

adom means red; it also comes from the word Adam, which means earth man or human being and from the word dam, which means blood. The red blood of the most important human being that ever existed, who is both Divine and human and is called the Last Adam, is crying from the ground in Jerusalem all the way to Eilat in Edom, to save Eilat and all of Israel!

For Zion's sake, I will not keep silent,and for Jerusalem's sake I will not keep quiet,until her righteousness goes forth like brightness, and her salvation like a torch that is burning.

Isaiah 62:1

The South Gate – Eilat Prayer Tower

Lift up your heads, O gates, and be lifted up, O ancient doors, that the King of glory may come in! Who is the King of glory? YHVH strong and mighty, YHVH mighty in battle.

Psalm 24:7-8

The City of Eilat, the South Gate of the Negev is a miracle on its own! Until 1949 when this area was conquered by the IDF, there was no city here at all. It was called Umrashrash and only a few buildings of an abandoned Arab Police Station guarding the border with the Red Sea and the City of Aqaba, which is actually the site of ancient, biblical Eilat! This is the southernmost border of biblical Israel and it is the South Gate to the whole Land of

Promise and of course, to the Negev.

Gates are strategic locations and it is of utmost important to possess them with prayer, praise, worship, prophecy and righteous acts in order to control who goes through them. Gates are places of authority. The Elders of Israel sat and judged the people at the gates.

Hate evil, love good, and establish justice in the gate! Perhaps the Lord God of hosts May be gracious to the remnant of Joseph.

Amos 5:15

Since gates are so sensitive in the spirit and natural realms, it is mandatory to protect them from intruders. It is like the door to your house! You need to lock it and let only friends in. It is no surprise therefore that most of the wars of Israel have started right in the Eilat area since Eilat borders with Egypt, Jordan and Saudi Arabia by sea. Every time that the Egyptians close the Straights of Tiran, stopping Israel's ships from going through the Suez Canal, it can provoke a war.

On the other hand, Eilat was also the place of signing two historical Peace Treaties: One with Egypt in 1979 and one with Jordan in 1994. It is no wonder that the Mayor of Eilat has the vision to transform Eilat in a City of Shalom, of music, sports and international conventions. Eilat is a bridge between Israel and two major Arab Kingdoms:

Egypt in the South and Assyria (Iraq-Iran) in the North. That is why Eilat is being prepared in the spirit as the connecting city for the fulfillment of the Isaiah nineteen highway that will bring true, lasting Shalom, peace to the Middle East! (See next chapter)

Enemies are always to be defeated at the gate, therefore the enemies of Elohim-God, the enemies of Israel and the enemies of the Sephardic and Negev restoration will have to be defeated in Eilat.

The evil will bow down before the good, and the wicked at the gates of the righteous.

Proverbs 14:19

With strategic prayer and intercession, prophetic worship and declaration, Eilat will be able to fulfill its purpose of being a gate of restoration for all of the Negev and Israel and a bridge of Shalom between the two major Ancient Kingdoms of Egypt and Assyria.

In that day, Israel will be the third party with Egypt and Assyria, a blessing in the midst of the earth, whom the Lord of hosts has blessed, saying, "Blessed is Egypt My people, and Assyria the work of My hands, and Israel My inheritance.

Isaiah 19:24-25

CHAPTER FIVE

THE ISAIAH 19 HIGHWAY

The Highway of True Peace

In that day, there will be a highway from Egypt to Assyria,
and the Assyrians will come into Egypt and the Egyptians into
Assyria, and the Egyptians will worship with the Assyrians.
In that day, Israel will be the third party with Egypt and Assyria,
a blessing in the midst of the earth.
ISAIAH 19:23, 24

B y far, the biggest miracle of all would be to have true peace-*Shalom* in the Middle East! Most of the news channels in the world are broadcasting day and night about the Middle East conflict! Mostly making Israel look really bad and as the culprit - the guilty party in the conflict. While Israel is in need of great washing and salvation, the truth is that the conflict in the Middle East is a biblical conflict and a covenant issue! Whoever comes against YHVH's land covenant with Israel becomes an enemy of the Almighty and will end up fighting Him and being defeated by Him!

O Elohim, do not remain quiet; do not be silent and, O Elohim, do not be still. For behold, Your enemies make an uproar, and those who hate You have exalted themselves. They make shrewd plans against Your people, and conspire together against Your treasured ones. They have said, "Come, and let us wipe them out as a nation, that the name of Israel be remembered no more." For they have conspired together with one mind.

Psalm 83:1-5

For they have conspired together with one mind; against You they make a covenant: The tents of Edom and the Ishmaelites, Moab and the Hagrites; Gebal and Ammon and Amalek, Philistia with the inhabitants of Tyre; Assyria also has joined with them.

Psalm 83:5-8

All the Arab nations surrounding Israel and all the nations of the world are defying the God of Israel Himself when they contest the validity of the State of Israel or any of its lands. The Abrahamic land covenant is in effect and will be in effect for 1000 generations or forever.

He has remembered His covenant forever,the word which He commanded to a thousand generations, the covenant which He made with Abraham,and His oath to Isaac.Then He confirmed it to Jacob for a statute,to Israel as an everlasting covenant,saying, "To you I will give the land of Canaanas the portion of your inheritance,"

Psalm 105:8-11

The only way for any "Palestinians" to remain in the land is by surrendering to the God of the Land, the God of Israel and not Allah! Other than that, they will be totally destroyed. But if they surrender, they will be greatly blessed! Until 1948, all inhabitants of the land of Israel were called "Palestinians" Jews, Christians and Moslems as Palestine was the name that the land of Israel was called since the time of the Roman Conquest in the first century AD. It is a derogatory name reminding Israel of their arch-enemies, the Philistines! Upon the reestablishing of the Jewish people in their biblical land, the name land of Israel was restored. The only name for the citizens of Israel be them Jews, Christians or Moslems is "Israelis" and not "Palestinians." Those that insist in being called by the name of the enemies of Israel are in great danger as described below!

Thus, says YHVH concerning all My wicked neighbors who strike at the inheritance with which I have endowed My people Israel, "Behold I am about to uproot them from their land and will uproot the house of Judah from among them.And it will come about that after I have uprooted them, I will again have compassion on them; and I will bring them back, each one to his inheritance and each one to his land. Then if they will really learn the ways of My people, to swear by My name, 'As the Lord lives,' even as they taught My people to swear by Baal, they will be built up in the midst of My people. But if they will not listen, then I will uproot that nation, uproot and destroy it," declares YHVH.

Jeremiah 12:14-17

This is exactly what will happen to Egypt, our "Eilati neighbor!" The Word of Elohim in Isaiah nineteen tells us how peace in the Middle East will be achieved and it is totally opposed to the political ideas of the United Nations and any nations! Egypt will have to be humbled and wounded before it will surrender to God's regional plan!

In that day, the Egyptians will become like women, and they will tremble and be in dread because of the waving of the hand of the Lord of hosts, which He is going to wave over them.

Isaiah 19:16

We can already see the signs of this judgment. River Nile is drying up and there is terrible hunger and famine in Egypt.

The waters from the sea will dry up,and the river will be parched and dry. The canals will emit a stench,the streams of Egypt will thin out and dry up;the reeds and rushes will rot away. The bulrushes by the Nile, by the edge of the Nileand all the sown fields by the Nilewill become dry, be driven away, and be no more. And the fishermen will lament,and all those who cast a line into the Nile will mourn,and those who spread nets on the waters will pine away.Moreover, the manufacturers of linen made from combed flaxand the weavers of white cloth will be utterly dejected. And the pillars of Egypt will be crushed; all the hired laborers will be grieved in soul.

Isaiah 19:5-10

They are now ruled by the Moslem Brotherhood; they are under a dictatorship.

Moreover, I will deliver the Egyptians into the hand of a cruel master,and a mighty king will rule over them," declares the Lord God of hosts.

Isaiah 19:4

They are suffering already but Israel will have to subdue Egypt!

The land of Judah will become a terror to Egypt; everyone to whom it is mentioned will be in dread of it, because of the purpose of YHVH of hosts which He is purposing against them.

Isaiah 19:17

As I am writing these lines, Egypt has moved some threatening military forces to the border of Israel, in Taba-Eilat. Though there has been a peace treaty with a "cold peace" between the two nations, the new rulers of Egypt are making it abundantly clear that they would like to change the "status quo" of the Peace Treaty signed by the legendary Anwar El Sadat and Israel Prime Minister Menachem Begin in 1979.

Changing the status quo on an already "cold peace" means war! Voices from Egypt have been claiming Eilat for Egypt saying that Eilat is Egyptian land! That of course is outrageous! There was no city here until 1949-- only desert and sea. But on top of it, the bible makes it abundantly clear that Eilat is within the confines of the land allotted to the Tribe of Judah. In fact, the borders of Israel are from the Nile (in Egypt) to the Euphrates River (in Iraq or ancient Assyria). These biblical borders include the Sinai desert that we relinquished to Egypt after conquering it during the Miracle Six Day War in 1967. We sacrificed Sinai for peace and now Sinai has become a very dangerous place for Israelis!

On that day YHVH made a covenant with Abram, saying, "To your descendants I have given this land, from the river of Egypt as far as the great river, the river Euphrates.

Genesis 15:18

It is only when Israel possesses *all* of its land from Egypt to Assyria (Iraq) that there will be true peace in the Middle East and the highway of Shalom will be opened!

We can expect in the days and years to come war with Egypt, ending in Israel, restoring the Sinai desert all the way to the Nile and extending its Northern borders from the Golan Heights through Syria all the way to Iraq, the Euphrates River.

> The oracle concerning Damascus: "Behold, Damascus is about to be removed from being a cityand will become a fallen ruin. "The cities of Aroer are forsaken;they will be for flocks to lie down in,and there will be no one to frighten them."The fortified city will disappear from Ephraim,and sovereignty from Damascusand the remnant of Aram; they will be like the glory of the sons of Israel,"Declares YHVH of hosts.
>
> Isaiah 17:1-3

Damascus, the capital of modern day Syria is within the boundaries of the ancient Assyrian Empire. Its present-day president, Assad is butchering his own citizens and the UN has done nothing to stop him. This is also part of the plan as Syria has been a thorn in the Northern Border of Israel at the very strategic Golan Heights, the region allotted to the Tribe of Menashe. So, both Egypt and Syria all the way to Iraq are actually suffering at the hands of their own people. This is YHVH's plan to weaken them so that Israel can inherit the fullness of the land from Egypt to Iraq and then there will be true peace and prosperity in the Middle East!

The oracle concerning Damascus: "Behold, Damascus is about to be removed from being a cityand will become a fallen ruin.

Isaiah 17:1

The land of Judah will become a terror to Egypt; everyone to whom it is mentioned will be in dread of it, because of the purpose of YHVH of hosts which He is purposing against them.

Isaiah 19:17

After these wars are fought and won by Israel, both regions (ancient empires) will surrender to the original covenant plan of YHVH to establish the people of Israel in the *full* Promised Land with no partitions and political divisions.

Once these two empires (Egypt and Iraq-Iran-Assyria) are humbled enough, there will be true *shalom*.

YHVH will strike Egypt, striking but healing; so they will return to YHVH, (forsaking Allah and Islam! *Dominiquae Bierman*) and He will respond to them and will heal them.

Isaiah 19:22

The highway of peace, prosperity and blessing will be established passing through the Eilat area, bringing untold wealth and thriving to Egypt, Assyria and Israel.

In that day, there will be a highway from Egypt to Assyria, and the Assyrians will come into Egypt and the Egyptians into Assyria, and the Egyptians will worship with the Assyrians. In that day, Israel will be the third party with Egypt and Assyria, a blessing in the midst of the earth.

Isaiah 19:23-24

What is the bridge city for all this to happen? The holy city of Eilat! The place of our Naval Base, the Navy Seals and the South Gate, the Negev and of all of Israel! The most strategic gate of prayer and praise in the nation! The true protection of Jerusalem!

Whom YHVH of hosts has blessed, saying, "Blessed is Egypt My people, and Assyria the work of My hands, and Israel My inheritance."

Isaiah 19:25

THE GREAT RESTORATION

The Negev is the hottest region in Israel from the climatic point of view. It is also the "hottest" area of Israel prophetically. It is from the Negev that Abraham established his sovereignty in the Land of Canaan, in the City of Beersheba, the capital of the Negev.

Abraham planted a tamarisk tree at Beersheba, and there he called on the name of YHVH, the Everlasting God. Genesis 21:33

In 1917, the Anzacs, Light Horse Brigade with soldiers from Australia, New Zealand, UK and others, freed Beersheba from the hands of the Turks and Islam.

The 800 men of the 4th Australian Light Horse Brigade looked out at the imposing walls of the desert fortress of Beersheba. Between them and their distant objective lay four miles of wide-open, coverless terrain – a veritable shooting gallery for the thousands of rifles, machine guns, and heavy artillery pieces that garrisoned this strategically-important city. Their mission was simple – charge forward, attack the town, and capture it intact. Blitzing on horseback towards a few dozen automatic weapons amounted to little more than a crazy suicide mission, but no one present on this day questioned his duty. Every man aligned on this fateful battlefield knew that this would be his final charge, and his finest hour. They were determined to make sure it was one that would be remembered for years to come.[1]

This tipped the balance in what became the British Mandate over Palestine eventually paving the way for the conquering of Jerusalem and moving it from Moslem hands to British hands. In spite of all the British Empire did to delay Israel's restoration, including denying immigration to the Jews escaping Nazi Europe, Elohim still used the British Empire as a bridge for the restoration of Israel.

We can expect in the days to come a great return of Sephardic Jews and *BneiAnusim* to the Negev.

And the exiles of Jerusalem who are in Sepharadwill possess the cities of the Negev.

Obadiah 20b

We can expect major wars (through the border with Eilat and Egypt and Northern border with Syria) to complete the establishing of Israel in its own land and bring lasting shalom- wellbeing, wholeness and peace to the Middle East, according to Isaiah 17 and 19.

---

1   (http://www.badassoftheweek.com/lighthorse.html)

All these things are dramatic and momentous and it needs all of our prayers for all covenant promises to be fulfilled in the Negev and for all Israel to be restored prior to the imminent return of Messiah.

Therefore, repent and return, so that your sins may be wiped away, in order that times of refreshing may come from the presence of the Lord; And that He may send Yeshua, the Messiah appointed for you,whom heaven must receive until the period of restoration of all things about which Elohim spoke by the mouth of His holy prophets from ancient time.

Acts 3:19-21

We are calling the nations like the Anzacs, to come and free the Negev through their prayers, worship, prophetic declarations, finances and actions and to prepare it for its legal heirs, the Sephardic Jews and the full restoration of Israel. We believe that many of the Moslem Bedouin squatters will get saved shortly and will become a great blessing to Israel!

The Eilat Prayer Tower is being established for this purpose and to protect the borders of Israel. Also for Eilat to be a city of revival where both soldiers and civilians can meet salvation face to face! We can envision prayer towers like this also in the City of Beersheba and the Northern Gate of the Negev Ashkelon and Jerusalem. The work is vast and the need is great! Yeshua is mobilizing His End time army for this purpose!

A Place of Revival & Miracles!

The Negev, Aravah and all the way from Ashkelon to Eilat is a place destined for salvation (Yeshua!) signs, wonders and miracles! It is very important to take Yah's Word literally before any interpretation is applied to it! The promise in Isaiah 35 is very clear and it includes:

- Salvations
- Blind eyes opened
- Deaf ears unstopped
- Lames healed and leaping like deer
- Mute people shouting for joy
- A breaking of miracle waters in the dry desert
- People walking in Holiness!

A Tremendous & Miraculous Move of God is on its Way to the Negev!

Behold, your Elohim will come with vengeance; the recompense of God will come,but He will save you."Then the eyes of the blind will be openedand the ears of the deaf will be unstopped.Then the lame will leap like a deer,and the tongue of the mute will shout for joy. For waters will break forth in the wildernessand streams in the Aravah. The scorched land will become a pooland the thirsty ground springs of water; in the haunt of jackals, its resting place,grass becomes reeds and rushes. A highway will be there, a roadway,and it will be called the Highway of Holiness. The unclean will not travel on it, but it will be for him who walks that way, and fools will not wander on it.

Isaiah 35:4-8

We invite you to join the army of restoration!

"For Zion's sake, I will not keep silent"

Isaiah 62:1

Your Israeli friend,
Archbishop Dominiquae Bierman
Founder and Director
Kad-Esh MAP Ministries | www.kad-esh.org | info@kad-esh.org
United Nations for Israel | www.unitednationsforisrael.org
52 Tuscan Way, Ste 202-412, 32092 St. Augustine Florida, USA
+1-972-301-7087

APPENDIX A

ANTI-AMALEK PROPHETIC PRAYER DECLARATIONS

Since you did not obey the voice of Adonai and did not execute
His fierce wrath on Amalek, so Adonai has done
this to you today.
1 Samuel 28:18

Declare Morning and Night and as many times as you feel led to
during the day!

Abba Shebashamayim (Father in Heaven) Mighty ELOHIM,
YHVH Tzva'ot (Lord of Hosts) we declare that You have a
battle with Amalek from generation to generation and we
ask You to do this battle today in our generation, that You
may blot out the name of Amalek from under heaven!

Hineni (here I am) Yahveh to wage war against Amalek that has been very wicked in attacking our lives and Israel from the rear and sneaking against the weak, the children, the women, and all our weak places. Our battle is not against flesh and blood and we wage Your war against Amalek with the spiritual weapons of prayer, fasting, and praise. You are fighting this battle and we say, 'let Yahveh arise and let all Your enemies, the Amalekites, and all their friends and allies be scattered seven ways away from us, from Your bride and from Israel in Yeshua's mighty name!' YHVH we ask You to execute Your fierce wrath against Amalek today and we execute Your fierce wrath against Amalek today. We totally annihilate and destroy you Amalek from all of our lives, families, affairs, finances ministries, congregations, and all of Israel in Yeshua's name! We declare that we will pursue and we will surely overtake and recover all that you have stolen Amalek! With the two-edged sword (the Word of God) in our hands and the High Praises of ELOHIM in our mouths, we bind you Amalek with chains and all your friends and allies with fetters of iron – we inflict the punishment and execute the judgment and vengeance that is already written against you Amalek, today! In Yeshua's name. We recover all the souls that have fallen prey to you Amalek in replacement theology Christianity! We recover all the Land of Israel that has been stolen through the false Oslo Accords and "Land for peace" agreements – for You YHVH have a Land Covenant with Israel up to 1,000 generations! We recover all the wealth that has been stolen due to anti-Semitism, anti-Judaism, and persecution against the Jews through Christian Crusades, Spanish Inquisition, Pogroms, the Nazi Shoa (Holocaust) and the like!

We pursue, we overtake, and we recover all territory stolen in our lives, our families, and our ministries, (name your ministry), UNIFY and Kad-Esh MAP Ministries. We break your power Amalek in every congregation of the living YHVH in Israel and in all nations due to the deception of replacement theology! We uproot replacement theology in all of our lives, ministries, and all over the body of Messiah that the very name of Amalek and replacement theology will be blotted out of the face of the earth and under heaven. We recover all the believers captive in replacement theology in Yeshua's mighty name!

We uproot and destroy you Amalek in our finances, our health, our children, and our marriages! We execute YHVH's fierce wrath against you Amalek in every area of our lives and ministries! We execute YHVH's fierce wrath and total annihilation on all Amalek-induced diseases such as Lyme disease, fibromyalgia, cancer, heart disease, blood pressure, diabetes, dementia, MS, Parkinson's, depression, bipolar disorder, COVID-19, ADHD, schizophrenia (and all their derivatives) that attack the weak places of the human being!

We execute the fierce wrath of YHVH against you Amalek throughout the Land of Israel (and my city and nation) uprooting all terror, hidden terror, terror cells in Gaza, Samaria, Judea and all Israeli territory from the River Nile in Egypt to the Great Euphrates River in Iraq to the Mediterranean Sea.

YHVH, You pursue Amalek and all his friends with Your storm and fill their faces with shame that everyone will know that Your name, YHVH ELOHIM, is the Most High over all the earth! We execute Your fierce wrath against Amalek in the government of the Church and of our Nation [your country], and every nation represented in the United Nations for Israel and we take back our governments and nations to become Sheep Nations, worshippers of Yeshua and lovers of Israel!

We execute Your fierce wrath against Amalek in the United Nations and we blot out the very name of Amalek and all his friends within every council and every officer anti-Israel or anti-Zionist in Yeshua's mighty name. YHVH, You execute Your fierce wrath against Amalek in Islam and uproot and blot out the memory of Islam from under heaven and we take back all the souls that have been captives to Amalek-Islam in Yeshua's mighty name.

YHVH, You execute Your fierce wrath against Amalek in all persecutors of the Messianic, Apostolic, Prophetic Jews and Grafted-in ones (gentiles) in Israel and in all nations especially from other Christians or Messianic believers that oppose Your End time Move of Restoration – including the

Yad L'achim organization that seeks to destroy the Messianic Jews that are true followers of Messiah. We execute Your fierce wrath YHVH against Amalek and every spirit of anti-Messiah in Judaism, Christianity, Islam, and every religion and religious system in Yeshua's mighty name!

We break your power Amalek in the Negev, Beer Sheva, Eilat, the Mountains of Edom, Mevaseret Zyon, Yerushalayim, Herzlya, Raanana, Kfar Saba, St. Augustine Florida (name your city here) and all over Israel and we leave no remnant! In Yeshua's mighty name we pray, declare, execute, uproot and recover all that has been stolen by you Amalek in our lives, our families, ministries, finances, relationships, affairs, congregations, nations and all of Israel and we take much plunder to advance the Kingdom of YHVH with abundant vision, provision, health, favor, and success in Yeshua HaMashiach's mighty powerful name!

Scriptural foundation:

Genesis 36:12,16, Exodus 17:8-16, Numbers 13:29, 24:20, Deuteronomy 25:17-20, Judges 3:13, 5:14, 1 Samuel 15:2-20, 28:18, 1 Samuel 30, Psalms 83:7, Psalms 105 :8-11, Psalms 149: 5-9, Matthew 18 :18-20, Luke 10 :19, Ephesians 6 :10-18

APPENDIX B

NEGEV FACTS FROM ISRAEL LAND FUND

Introduction

The Negev, meaning "South" in biblical Hebrew, extends from Beersheba in the north to the port of Eilat on the Gulf of Aqaba in the south, with Jordan on its eastern border and Egypt on its southern border. The Negev has a deep history. It is the area where the Jewish nation's forefathers, Abraham, Isaac and Jacob, looked after their flocks. It is filled with dirt, rocks and canyons, as well as breathtaking landscapes, waterfalls, caves, archeological sites, cities and craters. Covering an area of 4,600 square miles, the Negev comprises over half the land mass, or 66% (over 6,700 square miles) of the State of Israel. Its elevation ranges from a height of 3,400 feet above sea level to 1,150 feet below sea level.

Five different ecological regions fall within the area of the Negev. These range from the "Mediterranean Zone," with fairly fertile soils to inferior soils where little can grow without special soil additives. People originally thought the Negev was virtually uninhabitable, but as Israel's first Prime Minister, David Ben-Gurion realized "The Negev offers the greatest opportunity to accomplish everything from the very beginning."

In 2005, then Prime Minister Ariel Sharon restored David Ben-Gurion's vision when he committed the government to a project titled "Negev 2015". This incorporates a comprehensive $3.6 billion, 10-year plan to boost growth and development in the region, including infrastructure, housing, education, tourism and industry.

Critical Facts

The Negev is mainly inhabited by Jews and Bedouins. 14.3% of Israel's population currently resides in the southern part of the country. This includes 14.6% Jews. (Central Bureau of Statistics, 2007)

For centuries, the Negev has been 'home' to Bedouins, who in recent years have increasingly settled into more permanent homes and left their nomadic lifestyle. Much of these buildings have been done illegally.

Many Arabs want to use the Negev to divide Israel and connect areas of the Judean and Hebron Hills to Egypt and Gaza.

The growth rate of the population of the Negev has been negative since 1996 and continues to decline. National priority has been given to the Negev. The aim is to increase the population in the region from 535,000 in 2005 to 900,000 by 2015.

Many of the current IDF bases from the center of the country are expected to move to the Negev. This will have a positive influence on the development of the region.

Most of the land in the Negev is state owned. The land available for purchasing through the Israel Land Fund is mostly for agricultural purposes.

Southern Highlights:

David Ben Gurion, Israel's first prime minister made his home in Kibbutz SdeBoker, in the Negev. The hut he used to live is a museum dedicated to his legacy.

The world's largest solar power station is being planned in the Negev by Ben Gurion University together with the Blaustein Institute for Desert Research in SdeBoker.

The Negev has an arid and semi-arid climate with an average rainfall of between 2-6 inches annually.

Israel, through the Negev, is internationally renowned for combating the desert and preventing desertification of fertile lands. The Negev's water and soil conservation programs have become models in sustainable land management worldwide.

The Negev Foundation is recognized for its promotion of desert agricultural innovations.

In 1959 Simcha Blass, considered the father of modern drip irrigation, developed the first drip irrigation system to irrigate Kibbutz Hatzerim, eight kilometers from Beer Sheva. He was also the person most responsible for drawing up initial plans to convey waters to the Negev from 1939.

Unlike other areas where reclaimed waters are poured into the sea, the Negev relies to a large extent on recycled water piped in from Tel Aviv. This is used mainly for agriculture and irrigation. Saline water from underground reservoirs is used for certain crops and plants.

The Negev is home to high quality educational institutions, such as Ben Gurion University and Sapir College that attract thousands of students each year.

Four ancient Nabataea towns in the Negev have been inscribed on UNESCO's World Heritage List.

Farmers use the year-round sunlight and advanced irrigation systems to produce fine crops of grain, fodder, fruit and vegetables. The Aravah, on the eastern border of the Negev, produces over 90% of Israel's melon exports.

The Negev has abundant prehistoric remains and remnants of early historic settlements. These include flint arrowheads dating to the Late Stone Age (c. 7000 BCE). Tel Arad, in the Eastern Negev, is the site of a biblical town that is one of the earliest known urban settlements

The Negev's natural resources include potash, bromine, magnesium, as well as copper that is mined at Timna and natural gas at Rosh Zohar.

The Negev has six cities with Beer Sheva, known as the capital of the Negev, the largest. It has seven local councils and ten regional councils.

The town of Arad is popular amongst people suffering from asthma and allergies as it contains clean, dry air.

Kibbutz Yotvata in the Negev is one of Israel's major dairies, and attracts visitors year-round.

A prime feature of the Negev is its erosion craters (or *Makteshim* in Hebrew), surrounded by high cliffs. One of the best known of these is Maktesh Ramon. The craters were created by erosion of upward-folded strata or anticlines, together with horizontal stresses.

The Negev is set to become a world center of an important component used in the manufacturing of tires. An Israeli company based in the Negev, Dimona Silica Industries (DSI) has found a use for silica or silicon dioxide, which until now has been considered a waste product. DSI has developed an innovative way of turning silica found in the region from a solid form into liquid.[2]

2   http://www.israellandfund.com/en-us/info/regions/the-negev.htm

APPENDIX C

OTHER BOOKS

Order now online: www.kad-esh.org/shop/

The MAP Revolution (Free E-Book)
Find Out Why Revival Does Not Come. . . Yet!

The Identity Theft
The Return of the 1st Century Messiah

The Healing Power of the Roots
It's a Matter of Life or Death!

Grafted In
The Return to Greatness

Sheep Nations
It's Time to Take the Nations!

Restoring the Glory: The Original Way
The Ancient Paths Rediscovered

Stormy Weather
Judgment Has Already Begun, Revival is Knocking at the Door

The Bible Cure for Africa and the Nations
The Key to the Restoration of All Africa

The Key of Abraham
The Blessing or the Curse?

Yes!
The Dramatic Salvation of Archbishop Dr. Dominiquae Bierman

Eradicating the Cancer of Religion
Hint: All People Have It

Restoration of Holy Giving
Releasing the True 1,000 Fold Blessing

Yeshua is the Name
The Important Restoration of the True Name of the Messiah

Defeating Depression
This Book is a Kiss from Heaven

From Sickology to a Healthy Logic
The Product of 18 Years Walking Through Psychiatric Hospitals

ATG: Addicts Turning to God
The Biblical Way to Handle Addicts and Addictions

The Woman Factor by Rabbi Baruch Bierman
Freedom From Womanphobia

The Revival of the Third Day (Free E-Book)
The Return to Yeshua the Jewish Messiah

Also Available

Music Albums
www.kad-esh.org/shop/
The Key of Abraham
Abba Shebashamayim
Uru
Retorno

Get Equipped & Partner with Us

Global Revival MAP (GRM) Israeli Bible School
Take the most comprehensive video Bible school online that focuses
on dismantling replacement theology.
For more information or to order, please contact us:
www.grmbibleschool.com
grm@dominiquaebierman.com

United Nations for Israel Movement
We invite you to join us as a member and partner with $25 a
month, which supports the advancing of this End time vision
that will bring true unity to the body of the Messiah. We will see
the One New Man form, witness the restoration of Israel, and
take part in the birthing of Sheep Nations. Today is an exciting
time to be serving Him!
www.unitednationsforisrael.org
info@unitednationsforisrael.org

Global Re-Education Initiative (GRI) Against Anti-Semitism
Discover the Jewishness of Jesus and defeat Christian anti-Semitism with this online video course to see revival in your nation!
www.against-antisemitism.com
info@against-antisemitism.com

Join Our Annual Israel Tours
Travel through the Holy Land and watch the Hebrew Holy
Scriptures come alive.
www.kad-esh.org/tours-and-events/

To Send Offerings to Support our Work
Your help keeps this mission of restoration going far and wide.
www.kad-esh.org/donations

CONTACT US

Archbishop Dr. Dominiquae & Rabbi Baruch Bierman
Kad-Esh MAP Ministries | www.kad-esh.org | info@kad-esh.org
United Nations for Israel | www.unitednationsforisrael.org
Zions Gospel Press | shalom@zionsgospel.com
52 Tuscan Way, Ste 202-412, 32092 St. Augustine Florida, USA
+1-972-301-7087